THE HOUSE OF YOU®:

PRESCRIPTION FOR LIVING

By
Justin Alan Hayes, MBA

ALSO, AUTHOR OF THE HOUSE OF YOU®:
5 WORKFORCE PREPARATION TIPS FOR A
SUCCESSFUL CAREER

ISBN-13: 978-1-7349517-1-4

First Printed April 2020

For quantity sales, please contact the author at
https://www.thehouseofyou.com

For everyone who has supported me in my mental health recovery

Table of Contents

Prologue

Option 1: Immediate release to face an uncertain future the second I cleared the heavy industrial glass doors of the hospital.

Option 2: Voluntarily admit myself into a psych ward for an unspecified length of time to begin the treatment for my newly diagnosed mental illnesses.

It was after midnight on November 10th, 2017 in the Akron General Hospital Emergency Room where I, next to my new wife of just six short months, was presented two terrifying options that, no matter which one I chose, would alter the course of my life forever. I was being forced to choose between a path of uncertainty, or a path of uncertainty with professional guidance; like that was any better. Like they knew me and what I was going through. My personal nightmare I've been living for years, a story that they had literally just become main characters in. Perhaps more accurately, do I simply accept responsibility and own what was happening to me, or try to ignore it and hope to God I don't end up right here in a hospital gown once again?

Clearly this was a life-treating time for me, which had only intensified to an overpowering level in the last few months. Leading up to that dreaded day in November 2017, the magnitude of the situation, albeit invisible, still was able to engulf anything else in my life. No manual or "self-help" guidebook could inform my next step here. Until that exact moment in time, I was my own hero. I firmly believed that I could correct any situation that had gone awry. I could solve any problem, based on the facts of a life lived, up until that point. Rooted in what I knew, I could help myself in a way that nobody else could. And so, this one time, I quieted my mind, my bullheadedness, my hardened heart, my ego trying to push its way through and dominate yet another situation. I listened. In the stillness of the sterile room, between my shallow breaths and everyone's steady eyes on mine, I accepted that I wasn't ready to die. I finally accepted that I needed help. I chose the second option.

Think about the purpose of life and what life means to you, personally. Really think about it for just a second. Ask a family member or friend what they think. Maybe your answers will be similar, communicated with alternate words that hold the same meaning. Maybe they'll be so drastically different that it will spark a discussion of opinion and learning. Those differences, no matter how subtle or glaring, inform our unique point of view, and ultimately make us each who we are as humans. Even as I sit here today writing these words, and as you sit months, years into the future reading them, I am still no closer to finding the answers to life's questions. But I am much closer to defining the purpose and meaning of my life; I've found my Prescription for Living.

Chapter 1
The Journey Begins

Some have a straight and boring path; some are winding and exciting. Some are long, some are short, but each journey we embark upon is unique. And sometimes, that journey might spin you around and take you right back to where you started. From birth to death, we each have a journey in life here on earth. And on that grand journey of life, smaller journeys fill the map like underground roots slowly growing and spreading from a tree's trunk.

Every small journey within my life's greater adventure has been different. For example, even though I travel to my parents' house for Christmas without fail year after year, the elements within the journey are always different. The route itself is identical to the previous year, from the streets I navigate to the one traffic light glowing red every single time I try to pass. But perhaps driving my wife's car that day instead of my own or arriving a little late because of unplanned traffic alters the journey that time. The weather could be 80 degrees and sunny, or 10 degrees with a blizzard; the journey is the same, yet some elements are different.

This basic example illustrates how even the most mundane journey can vary from one trip to another. Last year, I made it to my parents' house for Christmas dinner without incident. This year, I had to stop for gas five miles into the drive, adding a slight detour and 15 extra minutes to the trip. Some journeys are stress free, and sometimes others don't go as planned.

It's important to keep in mind that as with just about everything in the journey of life, there will always be consequences in action and/or inaction as it relates to the decisions one makes. This is especially important within the context of one's mental health journey. Actively stopping for gas that day lead to my family arriving a little later than planned; while the inaction of letting the gas tank run dry surely would have caused an even later arrival time — leaving us at the mercy of when AAA (American Automobile Association) would be available to assist.

Similarly, taking action when I first observed my symptoms would have taken my mental health journey down a smooth and straight path; while my choice of inaction actually led me through a winding uphill course with many bumps along the way, eventually leaving me at the mercy of professionals.

As we all well know, life is not fair to everyone, and hindsight is always 20/20. Had I known the consequences of my inaction as my symptoms were building while my life was spiraling out of control, I might have made some different choices in the moment to ease into a softer landing. My journey thus far has taken me down some questionable roads — the map of my mental health journey is unique, winding, and frightening. Inaction has hurled me toward terrible losses and action has helped me cross the finish line for some pretty incredible wins.

The journey of life may be different for everyone, with no instruction manual or road map to follow — but we all experience emotions and react to situations. We can all help guide each other down similar paths. You are about to embark on another journey throughout this book, this time with me as your guide. Raw and unfiltered, I will share my mental health journey with you in its entirety. I hope that by the end of this book you will feel empowered to take whatever action it is you need to at this very moment in your own personal journey.

Chapter 2
Long and Short of It

Most of my adult life has been unsettling, frequently feeling at a loss for how I was going to continue living this way. Some of the most basic tasks such as eating, bathing, and even brushing my teeth had become a chore. My mind kept telling me in order to do *this* task, I had to finish *that* task first — usually things unrelated to sitting down for lunch or taking 60 seconds to brush my teeth after stumbling out of bed. Day in and day out, the minutes and hours continued to pass as I stayed focused on other things, constantly seeming more important than anything else I actually needed to do.

What were those other tasks? Now I recognize that they are mundane actions, but at the time I was addicted to staying ahead and in the know. I was simply checking my email, refreshing my Twitter feed for the latest news, and watching for notifications on my social media profiles repeatedly; to name some examples. Later, I learned that this cycle was a form of rumination, doing the same thing over and over again and expecting a different result. I wasn't fulfilled until a new email popped up, which I could open and read immediately, firing off a response to feel accomplished.

I think my mind was expecting some kind of prize or reward for completing each task, trying to put some immense value behind the satisfaction of closing out each and every app installed on my iPhone. If I checked my email 20 times a day, that obviously equates to 20 times the reward for me, way more than someone else who only checked their email once a day. I would be 20 times more knowledgeable if I checked the news 20 times a day, versus someone who checked once, or not at all.

How silly does that sound? Unfortunately, at the time, it wasn't silly to me. It was my way of life for years, out of touch with reality while trying to plan for any and all "What If?" scenarios that might hit me in the future. This also means that I was actively overlooking glaring symptoms of mental illness, brushing it all aside and telling myself it was all okay because I was just trying to be a productive person.

Mental health and mental illness are things you cannot see. To the outside world, including your family and friends, one appears to be functioning normally, albeit a little strangely sometimes. Everyone has their quirks, right? Everyone is looking at their phones constantly anyway, so who's really going to observe that behavior and think it's a serious problem? Mental illness is not a bruise someone can see on your body. Its severity cannot be quantified as easily as a growing stash of cough drops and cold medicine in a cabinet when you feel under the weather. Poor mental health is not a measurable, visible thing like fevers or runny noses.

I can't even count the number of times I told someone how I was feeling just to expect them to understand. I was quickly overwhelmed because so much time is spent sharing and re-living the suffering of these feelings, when all I wanted was someone to help fight it. An effective and accurate diagnosis of poor mental health, and possible mental illness, falls squarely on the one suffering to outline every symptom, every feeling and thought empowering the problem behavior. It took me explaining over and over again with no new results to finally realize I had to thoroughly explain what was happening inside my mind in a way others could decipher.

A prime example of how mental illness was affecting me was that in all of my daily tasks, I was effectively transforming into a human *doer* instead of living as a human *being*. Underneath it all, I was so intent on doing *this* task, then *that* task, and then multi-tasking between several things — none of which were dire to my existence or personal growth — instead of just being present and living in the moment. By spending all this time, energy, and mental capacity doing things and worrying about the future, I had nothing left for my own wellbeing. I had completely overlooked how my inner thoughts and feelings translated into my day-to-day life. Why couldn't I pull myself back from the future? I was quickly hurling myself into a no-man's land, with no way to stop the spiral.

What I had thought was trying to be as productive as possible was actually a form of FOMO (Fear of Missing Out). My undiagnosed depression, obsessive compulsive disorder, autistic characteristics, and panic disorder were dictating my every move. I didn't know what to do to address each of them and begin managing them. Who do I talk to about this? Do I need to be on medications? Why don't I feel the joy of being with family or attending concerts like I used to? In the beginning, some of the symptoms I was suffering through could be swept aside, compartmentalized in my mind with the hope that they would just go away and I could feel better again. In reality, the more I tried to ignore and bury them, the more they reared their ugly heads and the more I wouldn't feel right.

I was a people person. I liked being in groups, I enjoyed presenting information to my classes in school. During college, I did more than my fair share of partying with a degree of alcohol abuse. Now I see that alcohol was my crutch, a scapegoat to how I was feeling at that time. When I graduated college and entered the workforce, I couldn't party the feelings away anymore. It just didn't make sense to continue this way of life, now with regular working hours in addition to random drug tests and alcohol screenings looming over my head. I had to be alert and on point all day, every day during the work week, which was radically different than my one-to-two 90-minute college classes per day schedule I was used to. This was when I became more aware of my symptoms but continued to do nothing about it.

I went from feeling alive in group activities to being uneasy and uncomfortable around others. Attending meetings rendered me physically weak, engulfed with anxiety and fear.

Meanwhile in my personal life, I was overcome with the same feelings. One evening, I was stopped at a red light on the way to meet my fiancé for dinner when the anxiety hit me worse than ever before. The seatbelt was strangling me; the air quickly became too thin. My heart was racing, my eyes could not focus. I was dizzy, suddenly paralyzed with fear within the enclosed space of my car. My fiancé had to pick me up in a random parking lot, and we never did enjoy our date we had been looking forward to that night. This particular event scared me so much I couldn't bring myself to drive anymore, even though I had been driving for at least 20 years prior.

Lived experience like this has shown me what I'm capable of. It has shown me how mental illness affects not only a person, but the people around them. Even after what I thought was planning for the future, staying completely prepared for anything life throws at me, my life still came crashing down around me. At the time, I didn't know if I wanted to continue living — if I *could* live with myself, with my choices, with my extreme lack of hygiene and appetite.

Not only did I live, I started to recover at a steady pace. All symptoms have since lessened, and I am thriving. If you are reading this for yourself or someone you love, I cannot think of a better person to learn from than someone with real experience. Those who teach about mental health from textbook studies can only share so much. Similar to traditional academia, the best instructors I had were those who taught how the real world *is*, not what they thought the real world should be.

Before we shift into the main content of this book, I want to make it clear that I am not a board-certified Psychiatrist or Therapist. I'm just a millennial man with almost 40 years of lived experience hoping to share his story with others. This is my mental health journey, a deep dive into how I'm tackling the stigma around mental illness and all that comes with it personally and professionally. You will be in the driver's seat, a witness to everything I've gone through to finally find peace and manage my mental health in a way that works for me.

Along the way, I couldn't have made more mistakes in judgement. Eventually, I reached a point where I could cry out for help or continue to ignore everything. However, without reaching rock-bottom, I wouldn't be where I am now. I wouldn't be able to share my story and help others make it through those difficult times, the tough situations, long nights and overwhelming feelings. I've found my Prescription for Living. Now, let's find yours.

Chapter 3
Childhood

From what I can recall, I had a pretty normal and wholistic childhood. I had braces (twice), struggled with acne, had a hard time finding my "tribe" at school just all the other kids. I liked Mickey Mouse, listening to A.M. radio, and playing outside in our huge backyard with my sister and neighborhood friends. We were the quintessential middle-class family, taking yearly beach vacations and perfecting our manners to become polite, good kids. My parents held normal, steady jobs. My sister and I attended public school with our peers.

As a family we frequented Cleveland Indians baseball games, always the highlight of the summertime. Some of the most treasured memories of my youth that replay in my mind are scenes from baseball games surrounded by my family and grandparents. Others are sunny and sandy memories of Myrtle Beach, splashing in the ocean next to my sister and smiling from ear to ear without a care in the world. We'd even take regular excursions as a family to Chuck-e-Cheese. I'd save up for months, proud of my heavy bag of quarters and walking in there like I owned the place. No other kids could match my high scores on Skee-Ball, I was *that* good.

Growing up, I spent countless weekends at my grandparent's house, staying overnight to attend church with them on Sunday mornings. We'd raid their pantry late at night because they always had the best snacks, too. My sister and I would snack on big yellow bags of Lays potato chips, passing the bag between us and swapping schoolyard stories. In the morning we'd dive into gigantic cinnamon rolls with orange frosting. We lived like royalty at our grandparents' house, and we very much enjoyed our time there.

Another bank of memories I hold close are my experiences with sports throughout my life. Just like any other young boy growing up in the 80s and 90s, sports were my everything. I loved watching them, playing them, listening to them on the radio — I soaked up everything baseball, football, and basketball for years. When I began playing middle school soccer, my competitive side really showed, becoming a very strong personality trait for better or for worse. Later I picked up basketball, where my team made it all the way to the 7th grade tournament championship. By the time I was playing baseball, my left-handed self-felt so special for being able to throw left-handed and bat right-handed. I felt different. I felt like I was better than everyone else. I was the cool kid on the baseball team… I was the cool kid on any team I played on, to be truthful.

Despite my larger-than-life attitude on the field, I really struggled with who I was off the field. Outside of sports, I found it difficult to communicate with others. I was very shy and painfully introverted. I was awkward in the lunchroom, feeling left out and lacking the courage to trade snacks or forgetting the words I needed to use to ask if I could join a group. In the moment, I took all of that great family time for granted. I felt different, and therefore less-than the other kids in my grade. I was good at spelling, attended church, and my mother even worked at the same middle school I attended. I felt judged, like I was the goody-two-shoes no matter which class I was excelling in. I thought that if I distanced myself from my family publicly, the other kids would accept me more and think I was cool enough for their lunchroom group or pick me for class group assignments.

Home was my safe space after dealing with days of stress at school. I found great comfort in my father, but strictly at home where other kids couldn't see me. He'd lay with me in bed until I fell asleep most nights; something I'd never dare to admit to the few "close" friends I had. Sometimes I'd wake up in the middle of the night and toss and turn until morning. I started going into my parents' room to sleep on the floor next to his side of the bed, this behavior continuing on and off for many years.

Looking back, all of these feelings and dependency on my parents/father were no different than the awkward puberty phase we all go through. I wanted my family to comfort me, and yet I wanted them to leave me be at the same time. Whether playing sports, attending school, or just being a kid, a sense of accomplishment, discipline, reward (or lack thereof), was reinforced by a combination of my parents, coaches, or teachers. The immediate positive or negative reinforcement was something I always looked for, because knowing if I had done something wrong or right was validating my actions, my attitude, and general feeling of self.

All the while, I craved encouragement and coaching from just about anyone who would give it to me, and yet it felt like the world was closing in on me. All I could do was recite the prayers I had learned in church, hoping for something to change, for life to be a little easier, to win the next game and do well on the next test — but not too well, I still had to show my peers I was just like them. I wanted to be the best on the field, to show everyone I was more than what they saw in class. I was a winner, a competitive kid who would do anything to win for his team and consistently come out on top.

As the years passed, this immediate feedback became less frequent, even though my reliance upon it was increasing as I matured. I should have been able to adapt to this change, as so many other kids do as they come into themselves as people. The weight I put on myself was quickly becoming too much to bear, the growing pains heavy and steamrolling every situation. My attempts to control my feelings had effectively caused me to bury some emotions and feelings, hiding behind my sports skills as my own way to feel validated. High school was approaching fast and furious, another roller coaster ride I wasn't prepared to handle.

Chapter 4
High School

Although I played sports for the duration of my high school career, I wouldn't say that I fit in with that crowd outside the baseball diamond or gymnasium. That bothered me in a way, it felt like a form of negative validation. What was I doing wrong? What could I change?

In the moment I honestly wanted others to change. I was already proving myself through my sports skills, so they should change their behavior and like me after practice too, right? I'd finally be invited to the cool kids' parties, to know their inside jokes, to be an actual insider with my own teammates. What I wanted didn't seem to matter to them though, so I searched for validation elsewhere, which led me down a destructive path as I began to form my identity during this stage of life.

After years of top performance in baseball and basketball in addition to following all-season strength and conditioning training, I entered high school with high expectations. To my disappointment, I was relegated to the Freshman baseball team — even with a laser-like focus on my preparation and performance. In basketball, I could see the writing on the wall as well. Not sure how to take these critical setbacks, I moved forward the best I could without a plan. Adjusting was difficult, especially for baseball. As a left-handed player, I was always one of the top starters on the pitching roster; even in summer league baseball between eighth grade and high school, I was a standout, doing whatever it took to help the team stay competitive and win. Someone watching the team unfold throughout the summer could easily pick up on my talent and assume I would make JV my freshman year. Making the freshman team instead of JV weighed heavily on me and greatly impacted my social life as I began what I had hyped up to be the "best four years" of my life.

In an attempt to bury these feelings, I convinced my parents that I needed to switch schools. Especially with the lack of respect and little to no playing time. Eventually they listened, and I was transferred from a public high school to a private school on the other side of town. I had high hopes for myself, both with sports and academically. Unfortunately, not much would change. In fact, in the back of my mind, I had hoped changing schools would open up the opportunity for me to start fresh with a new identity, and thus connect socially with more peers. To my surprise, the opposite happened. I still attempted interactions with students from my old school, hoping that the "new" me would be more appealing to them. Well, I was wrong about that, because countless times kids would tell me they had no idea I had even transferred and hadn't noticed that I was missing from classes. Talk about being an outcast! This made me feel even worse, my little self-esteem sinking even lower.

The "new" me didn't go over well at my new school either. Being a private school, it was very common for my peers to be trust-fund babies, the sons and daughters of high-society parents — doctors, lawyers, business owners, people with power and money. And so, with time, the crowd I settled into was quirky and unique. We liked to do normal high school kid stuff like hang out, listen to music, go to dance clubs and stay out late. We also experimented with alcohol and mixing cold and cough pills. The feeling of doing something "bad" that I wasn't supposed to made it all the more tempting. Even though I was aware of the risks of mixing those pills, the high and weightless floating sensation was worth it every single time.

As a direct result of this new group of friends and our extracurricular activities, my grades began to suffer. I landed in detention many times, craving that attention, even though it was obviously so negative. My attitude changed, and I became a smart-mouth, full of rage and ready to snap back at my parents for their comments about my lifestyle. I was having *fun*. I found my people and they were happy to have me. I was sticking with baseball, still attending practice and playing decent enough to stay off the bench most games. I was regularly lifting weights just to say that I did to keep the coach off my back. I would stall every day in season long enough for another high before practice or the next ride to an away game with the teammates who didn't care to have me around.

Suddenly, I was sneaking drinks from the bar at a few family weddings. I began to drop easy-to-catch fly balls in the outfield. I eventually had to have shoulder surgery which

I never quite healed from and my playing suffered severely. On top of the healing time, I was exposed to pain medicines. The surgery was supposed to help me pitch without pain, yet I never regained my velocity and throwing range of motion.

When it came time to take the SAT and ACT tests, I bombed both despite my attempts at studying with my friends, capped off with some pills to ease into the massive test prep booklet. I was drinking and driving, pre-gaming before the clubs with mixing pill types and downing alcohol. The moment I stepped off of the field after a game, I was back at it with my friends. Friday night football games meant more binging and loud music, rude comments to my mother as I stormed out the door, only stopping home to shower and change my clothes.

Within this whirlwind life I was living, my competitive nature was the star of the show. Being competitive in sports is one thing but being competitive at something dangerous and life-threatening is another. Something about me was off and I knew it. It didn't show physically, I had an athlete's build and continued to work on my muscle tone. And that left only one place it could be — inside. Could it be something mental? I had no idea, but all signs were definitely pointing in that direction. My competitive nature took hold in my habits, from the substance abuse to texting friends, checking email, studying, and completing homework. My heart was set on productivity and efficiency even when it affected my wellbeing. I was knowledgeable about a lot of things, and yet an expert on nothing.

When senior year of high school rolled around, my grades and habits suffered harder than ever. I knew I was loved, and my family cared about me despite it all. I just didn't want to admit it. I had found my way; couldn't they see that? I didn't need to be babied. I was going on 18 years old, the prime of my life! Well, my low self-esteem went even lower when I opened rejection letters from Ohio State University and a few other schools. I didn't know what I wanted to do with my life, I thought all I had to do was apply and they'd let me in simply because they wanted that tuition money. My sister was excelling in college, I wanted to be just like her — except with admittedly way less effort to get there. But was that what I really truly wanted to do with my life?

It became clear I was trying to satisfy my mental health by altering my appearance and behavior. I dyed my hair blonde, blue, and even green throughout high school. I started playing guitar, even taking it as far as playing at a school dance after a football game. A couple other students who were seeking a guitarist for their band approached me, and soon after we were playing small gigs together. Even though they were house parties, I thought it was great living life just like the big bands, Green Day and Third Eye Blind, while we drank alcohol, did drugs, and had multiple girls on our arms all night long. However, after a few gigs, I showed up for practice just like always. I knocked on the door, rang the doorbell, and called only to be greeted by the answering machine inside the home. I got the message. Another failure for me, leading me down a spiral of thoughts. Why is this happening? What is wrong with me?

To help myself make some decisions, I leaned on my usual concoction of pills and alcohol. At the end of senior year, I ended up heavily overdosing. That night, I took 32 cold and cough pills. My friend was just going to drop me off at home per usual, I'd sleep it off and be fine in the morning. Somewhere within the fog of his drugged mind, something told him to detour to the Emergency Room. He saved my life that evening. They pumped my stomach just as my organs began to fail.

After overdosing, I began a vague counseling schedule and took the prescribed anti-depression pills. I was still hollow inside, still searching for myself and the next step to take in life. I wanted to fit in so badly, and yet nothing I did was getting me there. All that time spent in my own head, continuing to ruminate over every decision and every activity, led to me falling back into my recent habits, my only sense of comfort. What was wrong with me? What was I trying to prove? What was I accomplishing with this behavior? I was hoping to find an answer by popping another pill or taking another shot of alcohol. Unfortunately, that soon began a way of life that continued well into college and into my 20's and 30's.

Chapter 5
College

My college years were hectic and chaotic. For a brief period of time as high school was coming to an end, I attempted to join the military to find some direction. My parents had talked me out of it, and my transcript, SAT and ACT scores could only get me into a select few schools. And so, Akron University it would be. Even though I could commute to campus, I chose to live on campus. I continued to not fit in, and I admittedly still wasn't surrounding myself with friends that would help me come into my own and thrive personally and academically. On top of this major missing link in my life, I had also lost touch with my faith, my spiritual needs being grossly unmet and leaving me with a moral compass that was severely lacking true North sometimes.

As many colleges and universities do, Akron specified that incoming freshmen were required to live in dorms that did not allow cars. Since a couple of the people I knew who were also attending Akron were commuting (not living on campus), my roommate was selected by the university according to shared interests on the new student forms we all had filled out over the summer. Eventually I realized that my new roommate was a thief, had a gambling problem, and was a drug dealer. It would be a common occurrence for me to return to our dorm and witness him actively completing a drug deal or gambling with friends. Once when I had found numerous brand-new boxes of shoes on his side of the room and no receipt to show they were actually purchased from the store, I confronted him about my concerns. This had all gone too far, and I was supremely annoyed, uncomfortable, and scared for my safety. All of this fell upon deaf ears, up to and including when I took my concerns to the university for help to remedy the issue. I ended up withdrawing from school shortly after the fall semester of my freshman year. With my limited selection of colleges, I was accepted into, and with no way to enroll before the next fall semester, I had a lot of time to think. Even with all that time to think and prepare for Youngstown State University the following fall, I continued down my destructive path that included drugs and alcohol — I was still underage at this point. That didn't matter. It was a way for me to fit in, to be accepted by others in a quick way to fit into the social scene to fend off boredom. No relationship with a girl lasted more than a few weeks. I wanted acceptance so bad that I tried everything, tried to be everything to everyone. My plan was backfiring at every turn though, leaving me to wonder why couldn't I control myself and the situations I found myself in?

By the time the transfer to Youngstown State University was official, I was a follower. I still didn't know what I wanted to declare as my major. I turned to my sister's major of Accounting because I was familiar with it and she was having so much success in her studies. I was good at math but had little idea of what accounting was and how I'd use it in the real world after graduation. I moved into my new dorm the weekend before classes started, and of course I made plans to go to the bar by myself — the one that notoriously served underage students. Apparently, all we had to do was show our YSU student IDs and they'd serve us. On my walk to the bar, I passed a girl sitting on a bench by herself, I stopped to ask if she knew the best way to get there. She said yes and said she was actually on the way there herself, and I could walk with her if I wanted. So here I was, a single guy at a new school on my way to a bar where I'd be undoubtedly drinking alcohol (probably getting drunk), with a girl on her way to do the same. I thought to myself, this is what college is all about, right?

This particular night set the stage for a good amount of my future in college. There was no middle ground, these activities became the new normal. I couldn't stop my behavior. It became like a drug I relied on, I needed it. Luckily during my second semester, I started limiting the partying to Friday and Saturday only. I stopped the partying during the rest of the week, but I didn't limit the girls. This behavior was maybe what some college kids did, but I took it to the limit, which was unacceptable and dangerous from a sexual health perspective. This narrative continued through freshman year, until I started to receive poor grades. I thought I wanted to be an accountant like my sister, so my academic advisor set me up to begin taking the required prerequisites. And so, by thinking I already knew all of the answers, I layered on the advice from other students about how to the least amount of work and attending the bare minimum number of classes I could. I was trying not to raise suspicion of my professors so they wouldn't be able to place me on Administrative Withdrawal.

This "advice" was being given by a couple of the other students who I was skipping classes and driving around smoking marijuana with. Looking back, this behavior is certainly laughable; trusting these people to give me sound advice. In fact, one of those students talked me into driving him almost an hour away for him to complete a drug transaction. Little did I know, he was actually a marijuana dealer, and I could have ended up being arrested had we been pulled over with this being discovered — since it was my car and I was driving. I think after this encounter I actually reconsidered my friend group. With this development, and with parents that could very well cut me off and stop supporting me, I came to a very serious and very real conclusion. I could skip classes, do drugs, have mediocre grades, and therefore not have a good chance at a respectable job if I dropped out. Or I could decide from this day forward that things in the classroom would be different. I think some of this earlier behavior was an extension of what had happened in high school, a continuation into being an outcast.

I don't know if I didn't want to mature, or if it was simply an issue of not surrounding myself with supportive people. It was foreign for me to even fathom thinking professors had my best interest in mind, and to take them up on office hours to begin building positive academic relationships. It was at this point something resonated inside of me. The change in mindset in the classroom was a welcome shift. This doesn't mean I would ease through the remainder of college with straight A's surrounded by the best people, but instead I would start combing through my academics with a renewed purpose.

Up until this point for me, college had absolutely nothing to do with the education and classes themselves, it was partying and girls, with academic performance as a distant third-place option. I began taking my academics seriously, even though I may not have had the best plan of what I wanted to do after graduation. When I actually started attending the classes I was enrolled in, I looked for ways to gain an edge in the classroom. Eventually, I crossed paths with another student, an Exercise Science major and former member of the U.S. Armed Forces, an older and non-traditional student. He started to lay out his ideas for how to be mentally sharp in the classroom with increased energy and stamina outside of class. His methodology was fueled by eating lots of salmon and daily supplements like flax seed oil, sea salt dissolved in water, and apple cider vinegar. My acquaintance gave me the daily amounts of each to take, and so I ran to the nearest health foods store and purchased the ingredients. Immediately I began to see results. I was more alert in class, actually remembering what the lectures were about. I even started performing better on exams, quizzes, and even starting to take the lead on group projects. My faith and trust in my new regimen and acquaintance put me in a good place.

This quick-fix mentality would continue throughout college and beyond, even until today, where I would research vitamins, herbs, and minerals that could potentially keep me operating at a high level and give me an edge up on others. I would use this "edge" against others in class, at job interviews, into my professional career, and later into my entrepreneurial career. While certain regimens seemed to work in college, I wouldn't remain satisfied. I was always looking for something else to add to my regimen. The best and most reliable quick fix was to eat less, because I wanted to keep a certain image and being thin seemed like the best way to keep friends, especially girls. This was a very powerful flaw that I was starting to believe as truth. A truly distorted way of thinking, for sure. I had little in terms of spiritual "food" nourishing me, so with that lacking, I only had what I felt others liked to guide my decisions.

However, despite all of these new regimens and diet (or lack thereof), my mindset about alcohol and partying went completely unchecked. I went overboard by thinking that if I walked to parties, I was doing my body some good by staying active. Walking to and from gatherings wasn't necessarily a bad choice at first, but it slowly transitioned into a negative situation when I added drinking prior to leaving when the distance to the party was short. This behavior continued even after graduation, when my alcohol abuse would become the center of my life.

Chapter 6
College Continued

Between semesters and during the summer, I worked at a local golf course as part of their course maintenance team. Throughout my time there, I had much-needed structure in terms of working hours. For the most part, my hours were 6:30am - 2:30pm on weekdays, with an additional partial workday on the weekends. Working at the golf course with a bunch of guys brought with it a lot of pranks, like throwing new workers into the lakes on the property, and even putting a dead fish in our manager's truck to bake in the sun. This banter and behavior was a short respite from the long, hot and sweaty summer days of mowing greens, tree and flower planting, and raking bunkers. However, my negative behavior outside of summer work continued down the path of no return, with some nights including trips to the bar and showing up at work the following day hungover. I didn't think twice about what I was doing to myself, I wanted to be cool and fit in, and so I continued.

Sometimes when all of us had the weekend off, we'd venture out to Windsor, Canada to drink and party, picking up as many girls as we could. Canada made this all the easier, since we still were underage in the states, and their laws were different. After a particular long night out in Canada, we all returned home sleep-deprived and hungover. When we arrived home, I turned back around to drive two hours to meet up with a girl I wanted to see. Not thinking clearly, I drove to her place and thankfully arrived without incident. During the drive home however, I was struggling to stay awake, finding myself dozing off while driving. At one point, I was in the right lane of the highway and fell asleep for one second too long. My car sped off of the highway and hit the guard rail, continuing on to slam into a cement barricade, totaling my car. Again, you would think this was the much-needed event, a sign, to knock some sense into me, but no such luck here.

When school was back in session, I was picking up a studying strategy. I found that I was taking the lead more on class projects and even becoming annoyed when other students in a group project didn't carry their own weight. I was transforming into a real student here, I opened up communication with professors when I knew my grade would suffer on a group project. I didn't want others to earn a good grade when they barely contributed or were missing from study sessions altogether. I was also picking up that I wasn't able to just sit and study or do homework for hours on end. I was operating at peak levels when I would alternate between 30-60 minutes of study and then 30-60 minutes of break time. This was part of my mental makeup that I think helped propel me, and helped me remember the information I was taking in. I was able to focus more and actually complete assignments outside of the classroom — and this was definitely a positive.

A particular experience is standing out to me as I write this. I was taking a Consumer Behavior summer class during this high-performance window. There was an upcoming exam that I had completely prepared for and felt confident about. I went to class on exam day as confident as a student could feel. Before the exam papers were passed out, the professor asked if there were any questions. One student raised their hand and asked if the class could take an oral exam, where random students would be called upon and quizzed. Individual points could be tallied into a pool for the class grade, and incorrect answers would take points away from the pool. This idea was put up for a blind vote, either keep the individually graded paper exam or switch to a class-wide oral exam. I wanted to continue as scheduled, especially because I actually studied for this! We were instructed to stay in the classroom if we had voted for an oral exam, and to move next-door if we wanted a paper version of the exam. I turned out to be the only one who voted for a paper exam, because I didn't want the other students to ride my coattails in an oral exam since I was prepared. Alternatively, I didn't want to earn the same grade as the other students, had they not answered the questions correctly. Slowly but surely, one student followed, and then another. A handful of students trickled over into the other room with me, ready to take the paper exam for an individual grade. Perhaps they knew that the class overall wouldn't be able to ace the test without me being there to carry them. Eventually though, we were told to return to the rest of the group because it was determined we were all taking the written exam after all. This was the first time that I remember where I took control of a situation, believed in myself, and led by example for a positive outcome. And it felt so, so good.

Meanwhile, my toxic behavior and partying continued after class and through the weekend between shifts on the golf course. In fact, I took this behavior on a study abroad trip to Italy, beginning with abundant alcohol the entire duration of the plane ride to Italy. Myself and a small group of other students were drinking so much that we finished off a whole in-flight galley kitchen's supply and started helping ourselves to what we could find in the plane — much to the flight attendant's dismay. I thought it was a great time, we were making memories together; and this was the one time ever we could consume as much alcohol as we wanted without paying for it. Back at home, my habit of drinking bled over into driving myself to the next party or to the next bar to pick up girls. This headspace clouded my judgement immensely, forcing me to completely ignore common sense. This ultimately led to narrowly escaping a DUI after leaving a night club one night. It was during this low point in my personal life when a normal Saturday night routine included drinking, driving to a bar, drinking even more and then trying to drive home. I was pulled over once for not having my headlights on, even though I had just pulled out of the parking lot and flipped them on in the middle of my left-hand turn — just as the Highway Patrolman was driving by. When I saw those flashing lights in my rear-view mirror, I knew this was it. I was caught. After I admitted to having a couple of drinks, I was asked to step out of the car and participate in a few sobriety tests, which I failed horribly. The officer asked if I had been arrested before, and I said no as they guided me to turn around and place my hands on the hood of the car as he searched me for weapons. He informed me that I was being arrested for driving under the influence and handcuffed me. This was a sobering wake up call for me, but only related to the act of drinking and driving. My desire to drink, party, and pick up girls would continue.

I even drank before my final presentation as a senior in my Retail Marketing class, during which I would present to a group consisting of a local small business owner, class professor, department dean, and city business officials. Luckily, I gave the best presentation of my life that day and really saved myself a ton of trouble. I was the team lead of 30 students for this presentation, and we earned an A for the course. This behavior, even after the DUIs, reinforced the message for me that I could subconsciously perform well, even presenting in front of large groups, immediately after consuming alcohol. This was the point I realized that being the center of attention helped me thrive. The drinking at least was a cover for my introverted ness and anxiety, which at the time I didn't want to believe was actually true. I felt that the alcohol was making me feel good and took away the pressure, whether it was presenting, being friendly with others, and even striking up a conversation with a girl I didn't know. It also allowed me to fit in easily with classmates, and it actually made me a master at telling jokes and getting a laugh.

Not everything about college was fun and games for me, though. Another roommate situation arose during my time at Youngstown that I now regard as a very traumatic experience. One of my roommates owned a handgun, despite campus rules being a no-carry zone. Up until then, I had never seen a firearm in person, so this was a complete shock on so many levels. He would pull it out and point it at things in our apartment like he was going to shoot. This freaked me out because I wasn't really a gun person, and knew he was breaking some strict campus and dorm policies. Plus, I never knew if it was loaded or not, so the danger level was immense. Incidents like this happened a lot, so I eventually contacted management and told them about the situation. To my dismay, they did nothing. So by the time I passed my roommate in the hallway later that day, he had already found out that I had reported him. He told me that we would talk about this later when he was finished with his classes that day, which I took as a threat. Especially knowing that he had been involved in physical altercations with other students he had problems with in the past, football-playing brother and some teammates in tow. Pair that with knowing about his gun, and I went to the University Police immediately in fear for my life. Starting then, I had a police escort to and from my classes and for any other movements on campus. I moved out of the shared apartment and into an undisclosed hotel for a time while the University held a hearing and concluded that his threat was real and swiftly kicked him out of his apartment and out of all on-campus activities outside of attending classes. After he was removed from campus, the university randomly placed me in apartments around campus until graduation, sometimes with weekly moves. The whole ordeal was traumatic, and the added stress of packing up and moving just added fuel to that fire. My anxiety flourished and my stress skyrocketed, and living in a constant state of anxiety was normal. Add into that paranoia, because I was always looking over my shoulder in constant fear that he would return and find me.

Despite all of this, and even with blowing my entire freshman year with no effort in class, I was still able to earn a 3.34 GPA, which was something I didn't even achieve in high school. This, after shifting my major from Accounting to Criminal Justice, and finally selecting Marketing, was a huge accomplishment for me. For a period of time, I was so stuck on Criminal Justice that I had the ambition of following through and advancing on to law school. I quickly learned through poor results on the standardized entrance exam, the Law School Admission Test (LSAT), that this was not something in the cards for me. At the time, I was devastated, but I was resilient in moving on to something I was better suited for and was proud of myself for not giving up on my dream to finish college.

At the time of graduation, I didn't have internship experience, or really any outside experience in marketing to support my degree. I think this made my job search that much more challenging. I was so focused on partying that I didn't really even think about exploring real-world experience to set myself for success in the future outside of the college-life bubble. Cue the added anxiety and stress here as I attempted to begin my professional life.

Chapter 7
Cruise Control

Why did I think I could power through on my own? Due to the fact that if I needed a good grade on a project or exam, I would just spend the extra time preparing beforehand, which led most of the time to a positive grade. This was different however, the more time I spent preparing and studying, the more burnt out I felt, the pure exhaustion part of my fuel to continue on. Day after day, the stress became overwhelming, so much so that I couldn't process what I was doing. It was here that I realized that simple activities and tasks such as these were capable of becoming such a detriment to someone's health.

Each task and activity independent of one another is not such a bad thing. It's when, like me, that just about everything that you do is a competition or achievement of efficiency. That was how my mind operated; with constant internal thoughts of "What If…?". What would happen if I miss out on an email or text message? As I apply to jobs to begin my personal career, the fear of missing that one important message was crippling. It's what we now call "FOMO", or Fear of Missing Out, that was beginning to control my life at the worst possible time! In addition to this, my mind was polluted with a sense that I had to complete tasks one after the other, on and on with no relief. This behavior is also referred to as "rumination". I was knowledgeable of everything, yet an expert on nothing no matter how hard I tried to stay on top of reading, email, Facebook, news apps, and more.

All of this left me with no leftover energy to focus on the things that really mattered, like my health overall, my family and personal relationships. This situation was simply not a case of "chilling out" and "getting a grip". This stage of life was a case of obsession, of a serious issue starting to come to light. No matter how many deep breaths I tried, time outs from stressful or overwhelming situations I took, my mind was operating on autopilot and nothing I was doing was shutting it down. Even though they had just moved back into the area, I flaked on countless family dinners and get-togethers to focus on myself and the latest set of tasks at hand. I was so selfish to those who loved and cared for me most, all because I thought that I had other things to do.

Spending time with family ranks differently on everyone's priority list, but for me, quality family time ranked at the very bottom, underneath everything else. What was the reasoning? The majority of the time, it was trivial tasks and other plans, like going to the mall to pick up a new outfit to wear on a date. Others, it was having to shop for more alcohol to make sure my stash was properly stocked to host friends. If not attending events that I previously used to find joy in wasn't bad enough — now even settling in to watch a baseball game on TV became difficult. My mind was in hyper time, not only when I was on my computer and phone, but offline and trying to do a leisurely activity as well. I noticed that the motion and lights of the TV made me incredibly dizzy. I felt like I was a second away from passing out on multiple occasions. Even when trying to attend a concert for my favorite band, I had to leave well before it was over because of the constant stage show lighting and loud noises.

Unbeknownst to me at the time, depression takes shape in multiple ways. My rumination obsession, newfound introversion and unreliability, on top of panic attacks, inability to focus, and general apathy toward literally everything in my life were glaring signs. In fact, I even began to experience episodes of fear at the thought of attending a sporting event or concert; activities that I had loved to do, once upon a time. Since every human brain is wired differently, I can only ascertain that the use of my computer and phone only exacerbated my anxiety and depression. It gave me a crutch to lean on, as an excuse as to why I couldn't go out. What would I do for that long without being connected via phone and computer? My anxiety-driven brain felt that these pieces of technology were just as important, or even more important, to me as a human being than actually being present with and interacting with other live human beings in the real world. Hearing the crack of a baseball bat as it comes into contact with a ball, the snap of the leather glove as a catch is made, and even the smell of hot dogs and fresh popcorn were parts of attending live baseball games that I loved the most. And now? They were not enough to get me out of my room.

I was simultaneously connected and disconnected with other humans. Although I was almost totally wired in all of the time, I still intensely distanced myself from others. By having less and less communication with my family and friends, I became short on phone calls and my speech became mumbled and disjointed. I spoke in phrases and one to two word answers, rarely complete sentences. I also shunned the idea of exercising to take up my time, that I once leaned on heavily to occupy my time. This was the result of equal parts fear of leaving the house, and general physical weakness paired with newly developed exhaustion. Add these to, of course, no desire to leave my computer or not check my phone for the hour-long workout.

Despite all of this, sometime later I ended up moving back into my parents' house in an effort to bridge the gap between school and beginning a career. That was one of the largest changes in my life so far, as it is for a lot of recent college graduates. It was a great way to save money to help me get on my feet with a career. I was lucky in that I had and still have an extremely supportive parents who wanted and still want what is best for their son (and daughter). After all of the mistreatment, missed gatherings, and short phone calls, I was still their son, and very happy to still have their support and generosity. However, this began the transition from doing what I wanted, when I wanted to during college;

to living with rules and rebelling, a flashback to high school behavior, now compounded with my recent lack of goals and constant compulsion to complete tasks and activities.

Eventually after work, I would sit in my room, safe behind the closed door and shut out from the family, Googling whatever I was feeling at that time and leading myself down a rabbit hole of symptoms. I was reading mountains of information and not soaking in anything. I would type "best vitamins for stress" in an effort to convince myself I was trying to get help. Webpage after webpage of search results screamed the benefits of taking a vitamin to counteract the symptoms of stress, fighting for my attention at every click. So, there I would sit, consumed by trying to define my symptoms and feelings day after day. I would do the same web searches repeatedly, sometimes leaving the house long enough to pick up the specific foods Google was telling me to buy. I was ready to try any vitamin and nutrient combinations so that it would hopefully cure me. Some helped for a short time, others, the majority of them, did nothing. Not only was I jumping from vitamin concoction to vitamin concoction, I also started to rely on them instead of actually eating food. Most days I would sleep until 10 or 11am, tired from malnutrition and still not ready to eat a small lunch until the middle of the afternoon. So, there it was, half the day gone and consuming only 100-400 calories. For reference, the recommended calorie intake for men is 2,000 to 2,200 calories per day. No wonder why I was exhausted.

At this point, my computer and phone use skyrocketed well into the night and every weekend because I was determined to find the source of my symptoms and how to help them. At the same time though, I was insanely quick in dismissing professional-help websites. I refused to believe that I may have a mental condition that might soon end my life. And because of this, I refused to believe that I was not mature enough to get myself help at this time. Of course, I could take care of my own needs, I didn't need my parents to check in. Not only was I searching to define my symptoms online, most of them not visible except for my weight and look of exhaustion, I was having to constantly having to explain to everyone around me how I was feeling and what my symptoms were. I was adding the task of "making sure everyone knows I'm actually okay" to my never-ending to-do list. I began seeking advice from others, asking their opinion and thoughts on my situation if they cared to share. And yet, I never believed them. I never took it seriously.

Prior to my impending crash and mental health crisis, I was able to advance my life on a personal level by getting married. On our wedding day, the local newspaper published a picture and article about us on the front page with the title "Meant to Be - Couple is first to wed in St. Mary since 2015 fire." The fire destroyed several areas of our church, including the front where a chapel had previously housed the National Shrine to St. Dymphna, the patron saint of mental and emotional disorders. Now looking back, I can't help but wonder if everything I have been through up to and including publishing this book is somehow related to that fire in 2015. Like the fire at the church, a fire tore through my mental health and emotional wellbeing — and just like the church, I had made it through and come out on the other side. During the wedding ceremony and reception, I was in the process of breaking down. I felt completely embarrassed inside to my wife, her family, and my family as well. No amount of planning could help me not to break down, not to mention the passing of my grandmother during the week of my wedding, as if I wasn't already working against a stacked deck of cards already. I felt zombie-like with the patchwork of medicine my Family Physical had prescribed just a couple weeks prior to the ceremony.

I wasn't in the best frame of mind already, and the medicine took me away from reality in that I wasn't able to grieve her loss because the wedding had to go on; and instead of delaying what was to be two weeks in paradise for a Honeymoon, the memorial service for my grandma was delayed instead so that we could attend just hours after our return. Although that point in my life was chaotic to say the least, I was still able to get married and my wife put up with me during that time, as well as the full-blown crash and crisis that was still to come. She could have walked away and not married my complicated self, but I'm eternally grateful she stuck by me, even though at times life for immensely tough for the both of us.

So despite it all throughout this time in my life, I managed to balance my job and personal relationships throughout my 20's and early 30's. I kept my family just close enough, but bailed when I couldn't take the interactions any longer. Plus, there was a pretty serious sequence of events that happened in rapid succession: 1) A job resignation from a toxic company, 2) Deteriorating health of my grandmother (which I admittedly refused to acknowledge at the time), 3) A series of health concerns with my brother-in-law, 4) Moving in with my fiancé, and 5) Our wedding day. All of this took my anxiety and depression from bad to worse. Sure, I was happy with my new wife, after leaving a toxic job, and excited that my brother-in-law got the treatment he needed. But none of this could cure me. I expected everyone to realize that these 5 huge events were the icing on a very complex internal freshly baked cake. I was sick, and I never actually communicated my true feelings, even when I had the opportunity to open up.

One of the times on my recovery journey I knew I was left on this Earth was for the birth of my daughter. While she was born, and when I first held her, everything changed for the better. It didn't matter that my wife and I spent an entire Christmas in the hospital, the fact that our daughter was born just after midnight on December 26th made it all worth it. I wouldn't have had it any other way. Both my wife and baby girl were healthy, which were the only things that mattered. We would read to our baby almost every night throughout my wife's pregnancy, and so when she was born, I could tell she already recognized my voice which was the most joyful thing I've ever felt in life.

So now, having a child to love, care for, and teach, it was easy to want to help both others I know or don't know. As you may or may not know, taking care of a newborn child is not easy and it takes a lot of energy and time away from hobbies you've gotten accustomed to doing pre-baby. I enjoy being able to spend time with her, whether it is reading her favorite book for the 10th time that day, changing her diapers, or watching her get so excited to hear the Sesame Street or Mr. Rogers Neighborhood theme songs on tv. Part of my Prescription for Living is my daughter. She gives my life purpose every day, especially those days I may be hard to deal with. I can leave a bad day at work to walk in the door and feel her love for me helping me forget what had just happened. And that also fuels me to want to keep making a living to support my wife and our most prized asset, our daughter.

Chapter 8
Something is Wrong

The average person communicates externally to other individuals' multiple times a day in different ways. Some common ways a person can communicate externally are face-to-face with a gas station attendant, before or after pumping gas or after grabbing a snack, face-to-face/via telephone or e-mail to a coworker, or to the utility company customer service representative about a question on a recent bill.

For me, I was communicating to my college students in class verbally and via e-mail, with hiring managers/recruiters for prospective job opportunities via e-mail & phone and to my fiancé/wife in person before, during or after her workday was through. I love to teach others and share my knowledge and experiences with them regardless of the subject matter, so having this opportunity to share my knowledge and experiences and what was actually was a major blessing and a curse all at the same time. Looking at my previously described fear and anxiety around interaction with others, why was teaching suddenly a curse, when it used to be something I loved to do?

To help my fiancé/wife supplement some of our household bills while being in transition of a full-time paid position, I was picking up any teaching gig I could. This included not only teaching courses in person and via the virtual classroom, but additionally leading a project to transform the course mechanics and content of a specific marketing course I was teaching in-person. The objective was to design the very same course for online students as a way to broaden our course offering across the United States in the near future. This project was a favorite of mine, except for the additional anxiety and stress it places on me personally. A good lesson for me that I want to share with you is that just because you like to do something, it does not mean you have to say yes when asked. You aren't a bad person if you say no, and more often than not, a similar or better opportunity tends to come knocking at a later time. Take care of yourself first. You can't help others if you aren't helping yourself first.

To my students, how I was acting may have seemed normal, especially to those students who didn't pay much attention in class. Deep down though, I was questioning whether I should even be teaching when I couldn't even manage my internal thoughts and physical actions of speaking faster than normal; almost like an auctioneer, rushing through important course material just so class would end sooner. I even started giving my classes open book and open note exams, something I never intended to do in the beginning. Plus, with this new structure periods would be shortened, taking some material amount of anxiety and stress away from me. Extreme? Yes! Could I help it? Unfortunately, not. I shouldn't have felt this way or provided such a subpar service both to the students, the University and myself mentally and physically. You shouldn't have to feel this way, especially when you are doing something you enjoy. I was doubting in every situation and setting. It was a constant battle of *"I want to teach as much as I can during this period of time"* versus my body and mind drain on not only those class nights, but even the time prior to class preparing. Good stress or bad stress, my body didn't know the difference then or now. All the body knew was that someone or something was creating a stressful event for it.

Stress and being uncomfortable was an understatement when breaching the subject of any type of job interview, whether it be over the phone or an on-site in-person interview. Prior to this time when I had any type of job interview, it was indeed stressful, but during this time I was incredibly uncomfortable and fearful. I was uncomfortable because one of the questions that always came up was why I left my previous job. Uncomfortable because the way in which I had left that former position was one that people say that they understand and would do the same thing, but in reality, they wouldn't. And that way was voluntarily resigning because of unethical hiring and day-to-day employment practices, such as poking fun at job candidates for the way they looked and management being all talk about backing their direct reports up when dealing with employees that needed to be disciplined. In addition, I was assigned merchandising responsibilities, a field I had zero experience in, with my management knowing that my background was in marketing and marketing analytics. Try explaining that, or even remotely suggesting the real facts as I have recounted, to a recruiter or a room full of interviewers. Or even yet, the fact that it had been over a year since that had occurred without gainful employment in the meantime. Now, just because I did not have a full-time work position did not mean that I just sat around doing nothing. In fact, during that time, I had writing my first book *The House of You®: 5 Workforce Preparation Tips for a Successful Career*, taught several college undergraduate and graduate level courses, and had helped my Dad with his Meals on Wheels route part-time. During this time, I would soon find out how my mental illnesses were not a setback. Instead, they were pushing me to set goals and achieve them. I learned that no matter how uncomfortable I felt, I was still capable of making an impact on others.

That is why after I published my first book, I wanted to share the news with so many people that could benefit from what I had to say. One of those such individuals was Coach K – Mike Krzyzewski, 5-time NCAA national champion, 6-time gold medalist & 1,100 career NCAA wins, Head Basketball Coach at Duke University. And to my surprise, he responded. I was able to impact the situation of sending Mr. Krzyzewski a copy of my book and handwritten note, but I could not impact whether or not he would communicate a response to me. Upon reading Coach K's response, I felt as though my work was having a real impact on others.

Some people have a tough-love attitude in the way their thoughts and actions are portrayed to others. My fiancé and now wife are one of those people. I understood her intentions were good by telling me to get up and do something and quit feeling sorry for myself, but this kind of attitude towards someone like me who was struggling everywhere I turned and in everything I did and tried to do, was hard to handle. I was being treated as though all I had to do was flip a switch and I would be all better; and that I was choosing to not flip that switch on. Trust me, if all I had to do was say "abracadabra, be well" to snap out of my funk, I would have. Unfortunately, it was not that easy. My wife didn't understand why I couldn't walk into a grocery store without freaking out, why driving was such a crippling activity, why eating outside of the home was such a chore for me, or even why I felt terror during interviews, teaching and attending a concert, so much so that I would do just about anything to shorten the time I had to be exposed to the mental and physical discomfort. Mental illness is tough and exhausting enough to deal with on a daily basis, and so is trying to explain how you are feeling and what you are experiencing to others since the only signs visible to them may be a lack of activity or quietness on your part. Mental illness doesn't exhibit the same visible characteristics to someone like a bruised ankle or a dislocated finger does. If this is happening or has happened to you, don't let it stop you from pressing on because the only person who knows how you feel is YOU! Don't let a friend or family member sway you or delay reaching out for professional help just because they can't see the warning signs. Here I was, an extrovert for a large portion of my life who didn't shy away from interpersonal communication and social events, now turned extreme introvert because of my inability to manage my anxiety, stress, well-being and internalized thoughts and feelings.

A person's well-being is defined as "a good or satisfactory condition of existence; a state characterized by health, happiness, and prosperity; welfare". It's safe to say that a good or satisfactory condition of existence was not happening for me. My health, happiness, and prosperity were lacking at the least and my happiness were nowhere to be found. Although I achieved some goals, I didn't feel the happiness I should have, especially after writing and publishing my career readiness book. That was a huge achievement and I should have been proud of. Inside, I think I was a little bit proud, but because of all of the other things happening to and around me, I knew I couldn't reach the point of pure happiness. A lack of social interaction with others outside of my immediate family and my students was the norm for me. I knew it was unhealthy to want to always stay home and away from social gatherings and situations, but that didn't help me turn it around. Especially since the reinforcing message from those social interactions to me was one of anxiety, panic, and stress. All the more reason to stay home and away from what my mind and body considered to be danger. Not only was I jeopardizing my own life when I got behind the wheel of my car, I also was jeopardizing the lives of those driving on the same streets. There is no other way to say it other than I wasn't thinking clearly. Remember, I could troubleshoot my symptoms better than anyone, even a doctor. Or so I thought.

A big hurdle I encountered was realizing the fact that my body was sending signals to my mind that just about everything I was eating at the time was something I was allergic to. Throughout the course of my life, I had no known food allergies. Yet here I was, now allergic to everything except plain hummus and carrot sticks? I went to see a holistic practitioner, someone who specializes in trying to find ways outside of traditional medicine to treat real medical conditions. Since I was only going to a general doctor and sporadic Emergency Room doctor visits, I thought it would be a good thing to see someone outside of the mainstream medical community because again, I knew better than the professionals. Part of the reason I went to see this holistic practitioner was that I didn't want a psychiatrist to classify me as a person with mental illness. I didn't want to believe I was one of those people. In reality, I was treating people with mental illnesses just like a large part of the world was and has been — with a negative stigma. I believed people with mental illnesses weren't strong people and because I viewed myself as a strong person, I surely couldn't be one of them.

So through and through, I thought this particular holistic practitioner was a barrier between me and what was truly going on with me my body and mind. As with all the other hacks I had tried up to this point, this one also fell by the wayside, bringing me one step further from the old me and one step closer to a reality that sooner or later I was going to have to address.

Until now at the time of writing this book, the way I had been feeling mentally and physically had not crossed my mind as something that should be considered as something serious like a heart attack, or a stroke. Eventually, some feelings, thoughts, and actions would come and go where I knew something was a little off kilter, but I didn't explore further. I thought what I considered to be quirks were part of what made me a unique person, and of course something that I could handle and self-treat. In a way, once I accepted my symptoms as personal traits, I felt close to invincible. There wasn't anything I couldn't solve or figure out on my own or with the help of the internet, mostly through Google or social media. That was how I boosted my grades in college, by studying, studying and studying some more. Determination and studying worked for me, so everything else in my life should work that way, too. Except, what was still going on with me that an alarm was slowly starting to go off? Visits to the Emergency Room were on the increase because I knew something was just not right with me, but each visit ended like the one before with no diagnosis nor clear path forward.

Was this frustrating? You bet! I was hoping that someone somewhere would take me and my symptoms seriously, noticing that my new-found personality traits were actually dangerous, and offering to help me instead of saying, "Everything looks good to us, so we're going to go ahead and release you. Just try to lower your stress level and get some exercise". That was what I heard over and over again from doctors and nurses. I will now describe what I feel are the three primary categories that best represent how I knew something was seriously wrong and deserved serious action.

I don't write these words lightly, but it is my goal to be transparent with what I have and am going through because I know that you and I both don't need any sugarcoating, we need the truth, love and support.

Chapter 9
Crashing

Of all the content shared in this book so far, this chapter is the toughest. This period of time for me was very dark and full of fear, of which consisted of things I've been able to overcome with time. As you are reading this chapter, know that I'm not sugar-coating anything here. It is important to give as much detail as possible, because you may not relate to each area at the summary level, but you may relate to some of the details.

Growing up, I was introduced to doctors by way of annual physicals, usually for sports and occasionally a cold or flu. Throughout my youth and through college, I thought there was only one type of doctor, so every time I felt under the weather or needed an annual physical, I ended up going to see the same doctor, our Family Physician. And every time I saw the doctor, I started feeling better a short time later after my appointments. Even when I started having symptoms like a racing heart with heart palpitations, racing mind and lack of focus, hypersensitivity to light and almost every food imaginable, the self-diagnosis and use of a multitude of vitamins, fear of being alone, extreme stress and anxiety in all group settings, low sleep quality, among others, I did what I've always done. I made an appointment to see that same Family Physician.

Just to be clear, I am not advocating to not see a Family Physician. What I am saying however, is that they may not be the best resource when it comes to mental health treatment. A Family Physician can be a great resource to start but should not be accepted as the only professional to help guide your mental health journey. Instead, seek a specialist such as a Psychiatrist and a Therapist whom each have specific Psychology education and experience with mental health patients. A good analogy is if you were having car trouble. You wouldn't take your car to a lawyer to diagnose and fix the issue, you would go to an auto mechanic who has experience fixing cars. If you see a generalist, you will get generalist results, while if you see a specialist, you will get specialist results. This was something I learned the hard way. I spent numerous visits with my Family Physician expecting to receive a Psychiatrists' diagnosis and treatment.

During my almost 10 visits to my Family Physician in a short period of time, I participated in just about every test they had. I had several blood tests and two halter monitor tests, all of which came back within range. While there were periods of time where my heart rate climbed during the halter monitor tests, my heart rate always returned to be within the acceptable limit as determined by the Family Physician, and therefore not a pressing issue. Still slowing down my breathing was difficult and taking deep breaths was impossible. I was exhaling more than I was inhaling, and this continued to be alarming, even though after all of the tests performed. There was nothing conclusive that pointed to any heart trouble. If anything, the test results showed that my heart function was normal. I also went to another Family Physician that focused on the Gastrointestinal Tract. All tests there too, came back normal and clean. During this same timeframe, not only did I spend a lot of time in and out of the doctor's office, I had several trips to the Emergency Room, where ER doctors ordered blood tests around major organ function and key electrolyte levels in addition to Electrocardiograms (EKG) and even a Positron Emission Tomography (PET), where doctors reviewed ingested tracers inside of my body to determine any potential internal diseases.

Still, with doctor and ER visits, the results were always normal, average, clean, and not showing anything of concern. On many occasions, I was simply instructed to go home and schedule a follow-up with my normal Family Physician. All of these visits were increasingly exhausting and frustrating, not to mention costly. No matter what I was getting tested for or trying to do on my own, my symptoms persisted. And yet, I remained hopeful that the symptoms were going to vanish at some point on their own. It was also tough in the sense that I didn't actually know anyone with similar symptoms, probably because they were also bottling everything up, due to the stigma around mental health issues and the fact that some of the most common symptoms are virtually invisible. No one should have to go through life day to day not knowing when or if the symptoms would subside, like the way I was living for so long.

On top of all of this, the timing was just around the same time as my wedding and honeymoon. At that point, all of the combined red flags I had been living with were kicked into overdrive as the wedding approached. I was now convinced that there was something seriously wrong with me due to the longevity and multitude of symptoms that were negatively impacting my life on a daily basis, that all overlap into a generalized definition of depression and anxiety.

Experiencing anxiety is one of the most death-defying feelings I have ever had. Anxiety for me lasted entire days and nights, overtaking my life. It felt like my heart was racing so fast it was going to jump outside my body, almost always accompanied by bouts of dizziness. Anytime I stood up to complete a task such as driving to the store to pick up groceries, I could feel my mind and body kick up into overdrive, causing the task to rapidly become overwhelming. It became so overwhelming that I stopped going. And when I tried going to the grocery store with someone else driving, I was okay on the way there, but the normalcy stopped as soon we would roll into the parking lot. Once I walked into the store, a grand sense of panic started, with dizziness and shortness of breath. On the days where I could make it through the initial panic attack of entering the store, the same feeling soon returned while waiting in the checkout line. Eventually,

I realized that these episodes were panic attacks, induced by prolonged feelings of anxiety. The panic attacks happened at church, at the grocery store, out at restaurants, driving, on planes trying to travel somewhere, at the front of a class trying to teach, and countless other scenarios. Panic attacks hit the fight or flight mechanism of one's brain and are tough to get out of. Slowing down your heart rate is a start, but in the thick of a panic attack, breathing is challenging.

The problem for me was that it felt like I couldn't take a deep breath, meaning that I couldn't begin a breathing exercise to bring my heart rate down. Not being able to take deep breaths was a problem I had that caused my anxiety and panic attacks to linger longer than they should have. Everyone experiences these things different, and I found that I needed to accept the way my body chemistry is made up, such that anxiety was something that I was going to have to deal with in a logical and safe manner. At my lowest, this was very difficult to wrap my head around because since my anxiety and panic attacks amped up my heart rate and how quickly thoughts were flowing through my mind, creating a tremendous lack of focus.

Another major symptom I was having was depression, revolving around tiredness, loss of interest, indecisiveness, withdrawn and quiet around others, and loss of appetite. At my worst, depression was extremely difficult to manage, and I don't think I was even doing a good job at attempting to manage it. Denial was a big cause of this, simply because

I didn't want to admit I was depressed. Everyone has days when they are tired, can't focus, or aren't interested in doing things or following through with plans, so therefore there wasn't something so wrong with me that I needed help! Nobody likes feeling down or like they shouldn't do something because it will cause even more deterioration in a symptom or illness. Depression is a tough topic to tackle, and it is still something that I'm managing to this day. Looking back at where I was just a short time ago though, I'm definitely in much better control of my depression and know how to manage it way better than I could have ever imagined before I received the help I so desperately needed.

At times, I would try to mitigate how I was feeling by eating a variety of salty and sweet foods and drinking a mix of tap water, mineral water, alkaline water, and Gatorade. When I would teach, I took the whole variety with me to class, most of which I would consume at one time during a quick break in the three-hour class. I remember thinking and imagining what my students were thinking about seeing all this, silently comparing me to their other "normal" professors, causing me great anxiety all over again. The judgement of what I did and how I did it, and the perception to others at every turn was just another rabbit hole my mind would wander down. That became another huge red flag for me, but I thought I could just power through. What I didn't know at the time was that I couldn't, or at least, I couldn't on my own.

It was after months of the same symptoms with no end in sight that I started to think, "Why me?" Why was I suffering, having to go through this and why can't I just feel better? Everyone else around me is living a full life (or so I thought), not feeling anything remotely close to what I was, while I was at a standstill as days and nights melted into one another, stringing along for weeks and months at a time. One day shortly after these feelings overcame me, I was frantically Googling my symptoms and many different health conditions populated the search results. I read and read, re-reading many articles that detailed my symptoms and health conditions, in a state of denial, not wanting to believe many of them. For whatever reason, I had the mindset that I knew better than anyone and discounted what I was reading. As you can imagine, the range of health conditions I was coming across was vast, including heart and brain related health conditions, and a variety of mental health issues. The entire time reading about mental health issues, I discounted everything because of the stigma I had in my own mind. I wasn't one of "those" people, plain and simple. I just couldn't be a person who needed specialized help. I was strong mentally, or so I thought. In addition, I didn't want my family and friends to know I needed professional help because I thought they would look down on me as a weak person. Being mentally ill would mean I wasn't a "normal" person... but what is "normal"? Is "normal" going through life with over-the-top anxiety at just about every moment of the day? My thinking was absolutely warped and that was one of the effects of knowing that something was wrong and that I was crashing, fast.

What I would soon find out was that "those" people are strong and quite possible some of the strongest people I have ever met. During this period of crashing, I was closed-minded on many things going on. My Prescription for Living is rooted in knowing and believing that I would recover and get better eventually. I was stubborn at first, but it wasn't until I swallowed my pride that I started to see the smallest of positive movement forward. Remember, if you don't believe you will get better, how can you expect others to believe? You are strong and you will get through this and come out even better on the other side!

Chapter 10
Surviving & Thriving

We now enter into a section of the book where I will cover the parts of my life that have been made possible solely because of my recovery. If I hadn't hit the lowest of lows mentally, physically, and spiritually, and gained a second chance at life, I wouldn't be here today. I was given another chance at life, and I'm here today in a state of highly functioning recovery. I'm a person who needs affirmation and to be told how I'm doing — my Psychiatrist has told me he's proud of me and helped me find the best steps forward. I know that one of the main reasons I'm still on this Earth is to help others. I have said this at various times throughout the book, but I believe it to be so very true and worth mentioning again. A lot of what I'm about to talk about will describe the high points of my mental health recovery for not only myself, but the people around me who are also included in my journey.

I couldn't do a lot of what I have and wanted to without a mode of transportation. At the deepest, darkest of times, I would travel in my car with a wide assortment of non-alcoholic drinks and snacks with the hope they would lessen the panic and anxiety I would have while driving. This was if I was driving at all, which I hadn't done for a while before my mental health crash. I had lost all confidence in myself as a driver, which actually felt for the best and for the safety of myself and others. This fear of driving held steady in my life all the way past the hospitalization and weeks of group therapy afterward. Today, I drive all the time, which has taken the form of my driving many hours on family vacations, and all points and distances in between with and without my family on board. What has been a hi light of just recently is driving sometimes, not all times, without a host of beverages and snacks. There are times where I will bring a snack and bottle of water with me, knowing that I'll need them later out of hunger — not anxiety. A bottle of water is for thirst, instead of stress and fear. In fact, I've driven to and from places without bringing anything other than the essential wallet and jacket (weather permitting).

A few short months into my recovery, as an attempt to get back at it and speak in public again, I booked speaking engagements at colleges and universities in the Chicago (IL) and Miami (FL) areas. Attending these engagements was to be a four-day trip that had me speak in front of classes and groups of people about one of my areas of expertise: workforce preparation and personal branding. Two of the groups I was going to be speaking to were the college students who had just earned certificates of achievement that would now allow them to continue to pursue their academic goals. How awesome that I was included in these momentous occasions! All of the speaking engagements were arranged prior through a shared social network between the teaching faculty and me. A lot of unknowns, new people which I had never met before, and plane, taxi, and train travel, all at a time when I reverted back from my iPhone to a flip phone with only talk and texting functionality! I took the whole trip as a challenge, which some could argue I may not have been ready for. Nonetheless, I prepared the best I could and did it. I knew that I wanted to help others, to share my story to help them fight adversity — and this opportunity was what jump-started my successful career of becoming a public speaker and advocate for mental health.

So not only did I speak to three classes at two universities in one day, but I conquered a newly found fear of heights while on top of the Willis Tower (formerly known as the Sears Tower). I even had someone take my picture sitting on top of the glass partition to document my success. I have since continued to speak to audiences of varying sizes, some up to 300+ per engagement, where I have used high-level outlines of what I intended to cover and taped them to the floor. I have learned that it's OK whether I want to use speaking aides or not. It takes some of the pressure off of me always having to memorize the topics and their order, especially with the added butterflies in my stomach. I no longer judge myself as harshly as others, since it only adds to my stress level. I am successful in that more times than not, but I don't; beat myself up over the times when I inevitably slip up. Nobody is perfect and I have learned to accept that about myself.

I have successfully filed and now have my company, The House of You®, and have registered my logo with the

United States Patent Trademark Office, which was a goal mine since the beginning of my speaking engagements years ago. This provides me with some more credibility, which leads to higher search rankings when people search online. The process started with filing an initial application, but I quickly found that I wasn't in complete understanding of what I needed to include. I found an attorney to assist me, and he helped to guide me through the process. I learned again that I'm not an expert on all things, and that it was OK to ask others for help, and I'm glad I did.

Throughout the course of my mental health journey and recovery, I've kept my eye on additional ways I could help others (gaining the trademark and credibility being one important step).

One of those ways came to my attention via email. The local chapter of the American Marketing Association (AMA) was running a recruitment campaign for select Board and Committee members. This particular email was of interest to me because I had been a member of this organization for a number of years, and the Board of Directors role that was available was titled VP of Collegiate Relations, which fit in with my passion for helping students. If this VP of Collegiate Relations board role was a fit for me in the eyes of the organization, then I was up for the challenge. I was called to participate in the interview process, and subsequently voted into the role! Things couldn't have lined up more perfectly since I would now have an additional platform in which to help others. This opportunity has brought me the ability to continue to hone my speaking skills, networking, and mentoring skills as well. Not only have I been the VP of Collegiate Relations for the AMA, just a short time ago during our succession planning for the next Board year, our current President had formally asked if I has any interest in becoming President the following year. I had known all of the Board members were going through the succession process, and so I too had wondered who she would have in mind. So now in the last few months of our fiscal year, I have taken on the President-Elect duties on top of my Collegiate Relations duties. All of that wraps up to include recruitment and retention of organization members and committee members, learning the budgeting and fiscal responsibilities we have for our immediate chapter, and how to report those findings to the National Organization. It feels so good to be recognized by someone else for doing a good job, even though I was already happy with myself for taking on the VP of Collegiate Relations to start with, along with my deliverables throughout my first year on any sort of Board of Directors.

In addition, I've also gotten involved with the local NAMI (National Alliance on Mental Illness) chapter by participating in the annual NAMI walks. As a walk team leader, I help fundraise so NAMI can keep providing mental health services to those in need of them in my local community. Helping others who are experiencing a crisis in real time is important to me, and I've found that involvement with NAMI is a great way to reach them with resources they need.

And so, now I've realized that the glimmers of hope, the rays of sunshine throughout everything have all been added together and have given me the opportunity to survive and thrive in life. Let's discuss the part of my life thus far that have truly given me my Prescription for Living. In 2020, I attended two important conferences I'd like to share with you. To follow is a glimpse into my routine and structure while traveling to one of those conferences, and how I continue to thrive while helping others.

Professional conferences are usually held in desirable locations, such as somewhere warm with a compelling array of dining, shopping, and nightlife opportunities. And so, traveling to New Orleans in March of 2020 was just what I had planned as an AMA Board member. Having completed a successful speaking engagement just a week prior, I had renewed confidence in wanting to keep my travel as structurally consistent as possible. This time around I wasn't lucky enough to have a non-stop flight to New Orleans. I checked in to learn that the first flight was delayed, pushing my departure time back a half hour and compromising the following connections. Then, I found that my bag was overweight, and I needed to throw out my drinking water to avoid paying a fee. Between rearranging my luggage in the check-in line and rebooking my flight, my stress level went above what I had planned for a normal travel day. However,

I was proud of myself for my quick thinking and decision-making process. My new flight was to arrive into New Orleans at 11:45pm, later than the previously scheduled 8:45pm. Again, another curveball with the new timing that was out of my control. I try to keep my sleep schedule as consistent as possible, which includes taking my evening medication around the same time each night. This change, however uncontrollable and the best the airline could do for me, immediately added stress as I was trying to work out a revised sleep routine schedule in my mind.

Eventually, I thought I was booked onto the wrong flight after the confusing rebook debacle because my destination was suddenly Orlando that wasn't originally on my agenda. I checked out the flight and gate information on the large monitors in the airport. I searched multiple monitors for a flight to New Orleans and didn't see my flight. The number on my boarding pass didn't match any flight information on the airport monitors, so I began to think my flight will just continue to Orlando after New Orleans. Except I learned on the flight in which my boarding pass had directed me to, once we were pulling away from the gate with closed, securely fastened doors, that the flight time to Orlando would be 1 hour and 52 minutes. So, in true Home Alone 2 fashion, I thought I was on the wrong flight. The ticket attendant at the gate before boarding told me that there was only one stop on my boarding pass, and Orlando wasn't listed as a destination. Later, I was reassured by a flight attendant that my plane will stop in Baltimore as expected and continue on to Orlando to pick up new passengers from Orlando on their way to New Orleans. Those passengers currently on board en route to Baltimore and Orlando to end in New Orleans would not need to get off of the plane at those stops. So, I sat back in a completely new seat that I hadn't previously selected and enjoyed the flight as best I could. At least I wasn't stuck in a middle seat. When traveling, anything could change, but I had prepared myself with my go-to Calm app and noise-cancelling headphones. As I arrived at the conference in New Orleans as scheduled, I was proud that I made the best of a hectic and chaotic travel day. I'm able to manage my mental health so much at this point that stressful travel no longer consumes my being.

During the conference, I was able to interact and socialize with the conference organizers and attendees in a seamless manner. I think this was made possible by all of the tasks in my recovery toolbox, and even in part due to what had transpired during my travels. At some past conferences, I was like a fish out of water. I would avoid joining groups and socializing as best I could, from the networking breakfast to Keynote presentations. Here, I didn't feel that way. I felt a little more empowered and social that usual, which was a great thing for me.

A side note here is that in the past, I would usually attend conferences with a co-worker or someone I knew from the organization. So, a person might correlate that to a more relaxed behavior, but that wasn't further than the truth for me. It didn't matter how many people I knew and was comfortable with beforehand, I wasn't taking care of myself and prioritizing my needs in a healthy way at the time. Now in New Orleans, I was attending by myself, with nobody from my organization, and I was functioning at a high level. Case in point, during one of my most vulnerable times of day for anxiety (at lunch toward the middle of the afternoon), I was able to stand on stage with my co-table moderators in front of attendees and focus on what I was going to say about my background and expertise, while each of the six co-moderators ahead of me shared theirs. This was huge for me because despite the time of day, my ability to stay within myself, and focusing on the task at hand I was able to keep my cool. I remember many times where I would focus so much on what others were saying that I would lose focus on what I was going to share, coming across scatterbrained and ill-prepared. I was and still am very proud of myself for this recent achievement in New Orleans. No matter how well I picked up a task or function, I notoriously struggled with feeling a sense of happiness or accomplishment — and not this time. This was a major win for me and my mental health.

I received the following statement from a student at the conference: "Thank you for taking the time to talk with us at the Sales & Marketing Round Table. I wanted to let you know I've already started to put together my portfolio and samples of my classwork thanks to the advice you gave us." Receiving this statement solidified my happiness at how well this conference had gone for me. On the final day in New Orleans, I treated myself to a visit to Bourbon Street, known for wildness and binge drinking. In the past, this environment would have presented a huge challenge for me, with a chance of relapsing into old habits. This time around, that did not happen. I stayed within myself, reminding myself about how far I have come and to remember my progress. I was happy all around because I was proving to myself how good of a spot, I'm in. The next day, my travels home fortunately didn't include a cross-country trip and I made it home to Cleveland as expected with no issues.

Like in New Orleans for example. I've had and continue to have great wins and times of happiness but need to keep working at my mental health. I, like you, need to continue to identify new methods of self-care to add to my mental health toolbox. Falling backwards in my recovery is a challenge I face every day, but I have the faith that I can continue recovering and helping others in any way that I can.

Epilogue

First and foremost, living with mental illness isn't a choice. I didn't wake up one day and wish myself to have multiple mental illnesses — but since being diagnosed I've chosen my path and how I will continue thrive and overcome adversity. I've gone through one heck of a twisted roller coaster on my mental health journey, and I've accepted it.

Acceptance, especially for me, took some time and it may very well take you some time to grasp as well. We are all unique in our own ways, and that's what makes us human, so never let someone tell you that you're doing it wrong, not healing fast enough, or not reaching certain milestones on your way to peace. At first during and after my hospitalization release, I hated the thought of classifying myself as a person with mental illness. Now, I've accepted my new normal and have chosen to share my story with others as a way to grow. Without my acceptance of mental illnesses, I can't say I would be so passionate about writing this book and wanting to help others as my mission. In addition, finding consistency at something hasn't been the easiest thing for me. I've since learned that consistency has multiple layers: first believing what you are doing is for yourself and the common good; second, learning to not let negative thoughts from yourself or others to interfere with your goals; and third, visibility into the alternative situations if you don't continue. How have I found consistency that works for me? Here's what I strive to do as frequently as possible to provide myself comfort and peace.

I continue to take the medications I have been prescribed by my Psychiatrist since I was admitted into the hospital during my mental health crisis. I was hesitant to take medications for an extended period at first, especially because my longest time taking prescription medication was after wisdom teeth extraction and my shoulder surgery. My recommendation to you is to really listen to your mental health team. They truly care about you! The first impression meeting my Psychiatrist was that he was rude, not compassionate toward me or my situation at all. And now through everything, I'm glad I stuck it out with him, and I couldn't be happier with my choice.

One of the most serious ways I was hurting my body was that I didn't eat enough calories per day and wasn't nourishing my body with a balanced diet. Overcoming my constant internal monologue that I was too busy to eat and allergic to everything was a challenge. In the hospital, the nursing staff made sure that I drank a full Ensure meal replacement drink at each meal. For context, one bottle of Ensure has more calories than I was previously consuming in an entire day. I continued that habit after I was discharged, dropping down to one serving per day as recommended by my nutritionist. Now, I can confidently share with you that I prioritize eating 3 square meals every day as part of my consistency routines. Plus, eating a balanced diet and multiple times per day enhances the effectiveness of my medications that need to be taken with proper food and drink. I know now that if I don't nourish my body, then it is impossible to believe I can continue to recover at such a high level and to be in the best condition to help others; which is the foundation of my new mission.

Abusing alcohol used to be a large part of who I was. That's no longer true. In fact, I haven't touched alcohol since months before my hospitalization. It no longer defines me, and it's not something I miss. When I'm out with others drinking alcohol, I pick up a sparkling water or club soda instead. At most bars and restaurants, they'll even pour sparkling water into a wine glass or champagne flute garnished with a lime wedge. I've explained my situation to more than a few people, but I'm now owning my thoughts and actions. My focus is on continuing my mental illness recovery at every turn. Gone are the days of alcohol, drugs, excessive prescription pills, and in are days of safe, controlled decisions that are nourishing and respectful of my body and my mental health.

Lack of sleep and a bedtime routine was another very real part of my mental health journey, and a critical consistency I keep today. After years of what I thought sleep was supposed to be, I found out that I had been approaching sleep all wrong. To only was I lucky to get just 5 hours of sleep each night, most nights I had an extreme fear of just closing my eyes. I'm not sure what caused that fear, but what

I did know was that I rarely woke up feeling rested. Some of that fear was probably from knowing deep down that I would wake up just as tired as I was the previous day. I also never prioritized sleep as part of my life for a long time, and I was never consistent with bedtimes or waking up around the same time each day. I didn't finally grasp the importance of a sleep schedule and really change my behavior until I attended Partial Hospitalization Therapy sessions, in addition to an evening prescription to help me wind down before bedtime each night. I thought it was odd at first, since I thought I needed the most help during the day and not at night. Through many therapy sessions, I became fully informed on the positive benefits of sleep and sleep routines. I've found that wearing a sleep mask and listening to soothing sounds via an app on my phone has helped me get a better quality of sleep as well. Heading to bed between 9 and 10:30pm and waking up between 7:30 and 9am gives me the structure I need.

Regular meditation in addition to an improved sleep schedule still does wonders for my mental health. Meditation used to be frightening for me, behind my closed eyes in a dark, quiet room I was seeing a shark attacking me as I sat on a boardwalk and couldn't escape. I went through so many meditation app trials trying to find the one that worked to no avail. After my crisis though, I've found that my mind is clearer than it has been in a long time. I'm able to close my eyes wherever I am and don't think about shark attacks —

even if my new app has ocean wave sounds. It's not the meditation independently driving my mind and thoughts, it's a combination of everything else I'm doing to be consistent and mindful. Just the ability to meditate is a great way for me to evaluate how I'm handling stress, work, and other things in life; helping me sort it all out in a peaceful and meaningful way. Similarly, I now enjoy listening to classical music because each song's complexity allows me to get lost in it and really feel the music. The different tones and melodies of composers keep me engaged in listening, a completely different experience than the popular music of today.

For a long time in my adult life, spirituality just wasn't for me. As a child, I attended church regularly with my family for years, yet never truly understood the underlying spiritual messaging and letting it inform my mental health crisis in the correct way. Throughout it all, I had always thought that spirituality was a part of each of us, but just wasn't my strength. Slowly in my late 20's I began attending weekly mass, even going so far as reading. With all eyes on me, at a time where I wasn't nourishing my body how I needed to, the nerves really kicked in. I ignored that red flag, thinking I was just in need of overcoming my newfound fear of public speaking during mass, even though I had previously enjoyed speaking in front of large crowds. It got to the point that even as a regular attendee at a busy mass, I would experience extreme symptoms of a panic attack. Now with all of that in the rear-view mirror, I'm back to attending weekly mass and even joined a men's prayer group to strengthen my spirituality and understanding of Christ. I've fully embraced that I need spirituality in my life to help balance everything, and it gives me peace of mind because I'm no longer left wondering about it and challenging others on their views. How else do I know this is an essential consistency to my mental health journey? Being removed from Christmas Eve mass with panic attacks for several years hit me hard. In a recent Christmas Eve mass, I noticed a man in my pew displaying signs of a panic attack and generally being overwhelmed before mass started. I let him out of the pew, and his mother told me that her son has problems in big crowds and suffered from anxiety. When he returned, I shared with him my previous experience because it was similar enough that I felt I could make him feel less alone. This was my first Christmas Eve mass in a long time, and I felt good knowing that I had helped someone through their struggle. I realized that I was now the one on the outside looking in at someone else's challenge, and how was it possible that they were sitting right next to me of all people, in a crowded church service? I enjoyed being kind and thoughtful to them, providing comfort and understanding in that moment.

Going to the barber shop used to be full of anxiety for me. Currently, I'm happy to include self-care appointments like getting my hair cut into my consistent routine. At the time, I was in between jobs and had an ex-coworker who attended the same barber. The barber had mentioned my friend asked about me multiple times, and I spiraled into anxiety not knowing what to say. Would he judge me for my job status? Would he think I couldn't pay him and not do a good job on my hair? Whatever the reasoning, it was a side effect of how badly I was treating my body and spirit. Now, I don't worry about what topic comes up or where our conversation leads, and I'm okay with telling the truth without fear of being judged. I've since made appointments like this part of my monthly self-care routine. I keep the consistency by scheduling appointments four weeks out and stacking with other self-care appointments like my monthly Swedish massage spa treatment. That way, they're all easy to remember and my appointments are each treated as a priority. I encourage you to find what self-care routines work for you and stick with them. Be present in those moments and enjoy what you are doing.

As you can see, I'm very passionate in being consistent in my own life and sharing my story with others. Part of what I consider a consistency for myself is helping others through extra-curriculars like attending seminars and conferences to speak about my lived experience. Now, it's time for you to find the perfect mix of self-care activities that make you feel your best. Slow down and listen to your body. I never used to, but I never won't listen to my body again! Nurture your mind, body, and spirit any chance you get. Take time to recharge and become your best self. You'll surely find your Prescription for Living in no time.

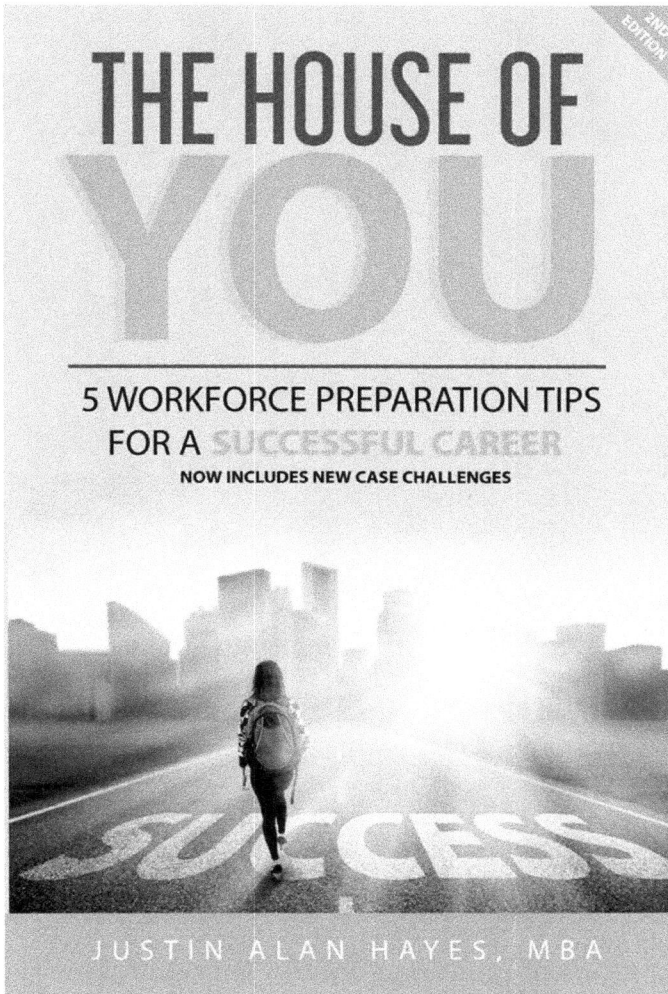

Also check out this title from this Author on personal branding, workforce preparation or transition.

Available today on thehouseofyou.com and amazon.com.

www.ingramcontent.com/pod-product-compliance
Lightning Source LLC
Chambersburg PA
CBHW062121040426
42336CB00041B/2159